HEADWORK
ENGLISH
PROGRAMME 2

Chris Culshaw and Jill Dodgson

OXFORD UNIVERSITY PRESS

Contents

Acknowledgements

The authors and publishers would like to thank the following for permission to reproduce copyright material:

Bloomsbury Publishing Ltd: extract from Ben Wickes: *Waiting for the All Clear*, (Bloomsbury 1990); **Chambers Harrap Publishers Ltd**: extract from *Harraps Easy English Dictionary*; **Commonword Ltd**: poem by Brenda Leather; **Russell Grant**: horoscopes from *Fast Forward*. Russell Grant writes for the *Daily* and *Sunday Mirror*; **IPC Magazines Ltd**: horoscope from *My Guy*; **Oxford University Press**: extract from *Oxford Children's Encyclopedia*, (1991), and extract from *Oxford Paperback Dictionary*; **PGL Young Adventure Ltd**: extracts from *PGL Adventure Holiday Catalogue 1993*; **Penguin Group Children's Publishing**: extracts from Gyles Brandreth: *A Riot of Riddles*, copyright © Gyles Brandreth 1991, published in Puffin Books, and extract from Brough Girling: *'Vera Pratt and the Tale of the Cow'*; copyright © Brough Girling, published in Puffin Books; **Random House UK Ltd**: extract from Michael Coleman: *Tutankhamun Is A Bit Of A Mummy's Boy*, (Red Fox, 1992); **Reed International Books**: extracts from Nicholas Fisk: *Grinny*, and extract from Willy Russell: *Our Day Out* (Methuen, London, Ltd), © 1984 Willy Russell; **Robson Books Ltd**: extracts from *Gary Wilmot's Big Book of Practical Jokes*, (1989); **D.C. Thomson & Co. Ltd**: horoscope from *Jackie*, © D.C. Thomson & Co Ltd; and **Wood Green Animal Shelters** (Heydon, Royston, Herts): extract from *Pet Ownership* booklet produced by the **College of Animal Welfare**. Also **Huang Wang** and **Michalis Mouzakitis** for their pet stories, first published here, and **Nick Welch**, R.S.P.C.A Inspector (Kendal), for the quotation about pets.

Although every effort has been made to trace and contact copyright holders before publication this has not been possible in some cases. We apologise for any apparent infringement of copyright and will be pleased to rectify any errors or omissions at the earliest opportunity.

The publishers would like to thank the following for permission to reproduce photographs:

Ace Photo Agency p.12 (bottom left), **Mauritius Bildagentur/Ace Photo Agency** p.12 (middle right), **M Bluestone/Ace Photo Agency** p.12 (top right), **Jim Lowe/Ace Photo Agency** p.12 (bottom right); **Bo Cederwall** p.12 (middle left); **Anne Farrar** p.60; **Sally & Richard Greenhill** p.8; **Imperial War Museum** p.38; **London Transport Museum** p.37; **Gerard Lacz/NHPA** p.58 (right); **Popperfoto** p.39; **Antonia Reeve** p.61; **Nigel Lumsden/Stockfile** p.12 (top left); **Telegraph Colour Library** p.58 (left); **John Walmsley** p.7.

The illustrations are by **Juliet Breese** pp.6, 23, 25, 35, 45, 49, 57, 60, 61; **Tony Chance** pp.40/1, 51-55; **Linda Jeffrey** pp.27, 29; **Pauline Little** pp.20, 21, 46, 48; **Jill Newton** p.22; **Rhiannon Powell** p.62; **Judy Stevens** p.10; **Duncan Storr** pp.15-19; **Marc Vyvyan-Jones** pp.26/7, 42, 43, 44; **Kevin Warren** pp.30-34.

Introduction

Dear Student

Welcome to the **Headwork English Programme**.

Each Students' Book is made up of nine short units. Every unit has a different theme, like holidays, games, food, or ambitions.

We have chosen stories, poems, scripts, photos, and pictures, as well as articles from newspapers and magazines, linked to these themes.

These are followed by **What to do** activities which will help you to develop a wide range of skills in speaking, reading, and writing.

At the start of each unit you will find a **Skills Panel**. This will tell you the main skills you will practise as you work through the unit.

At the end of each unit is a short **Review** which will help you to sum up your progress and talk about any questions you have on particular activities.

We hope you enjoy using **Headwork English Programme**.

Chris Culshaw and Jill Dodgson

Unit 1

Holiday

SKILLS YOU WILL USE IN THIS UNIT

1 Reading to find out information
2 Writing a diary entry
3 Drawing to provide information
4 Putting your point of view
5 Conducting a survey and presenting results

All Change

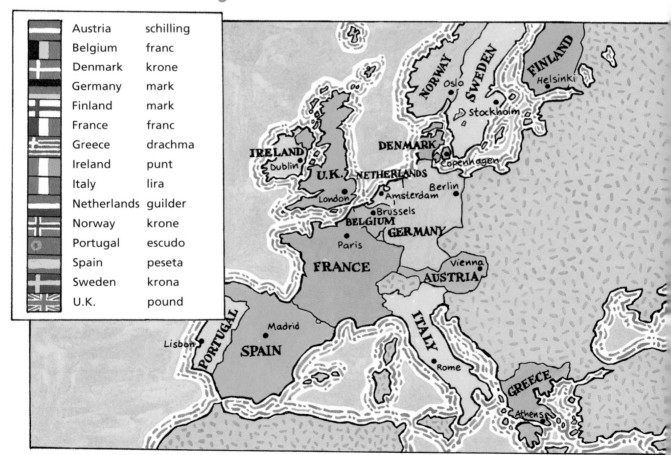

	Austria	schilling
	Belgium	franc
	Denmark	krone
	Germany	mark
	Finland	mark
	France	franc
	Greece	drachma
	Ireland	punt
	Italy	lira
	Netherlands	guilder
	Norway	krone
	Portugal	escudo
	Spain	peseta
	Sweden	krona
	U.K.	pound

In pairs

1 What are the capital cities of these countries:
- Greece
- Italy
- Finland?

2 What currency would you use on holiday in:
- Norway
- Ireland
- Germany?

3 In which cities would you spend:
- lira
- krona
- schillings
- escudos?

RATES OF EXCHANGE

TRAVELLERS CHEQUES		CURRENCY NOTES		Conditions
We buy		We sell	We buy up to £1,000	(We buy)
18.3850	AUSTRIA	17.60	19.10	20's & above
53.97	BELGIUM	51.90	56.30	100's & above
1.9358	CANADA	1.875	2.035	
8.8761	FRANCE	8.54	9.24	20's & above
2.5988	GERMANY	2.505	2.705	5's & above
	GREECE	343.0	368.0	500's & above
2424.62	ITALY	2340.0	2485.0	1000's & above
2.9227	NETHERLANDS	2.82	3.05	
266.33	PORTUGAL	251.5	269.5	500's & above
212.81	SPAIN	202.0	215.0	1000's & above
2.2853	SWITZERLAND	2.205	2.385	10's & above
1.5109	USA	1.46	1.59	

What to do next

In a small group

1 If you travel from Rome to Paris you have to change lira into francs.
Write a similar sentence for these journeys:
- Stockholm to London
- Madrid to Amsterdam

2 Find out the capital city and currency of other countries. Use the information to make a clear and attractive chart suitable for display in a Tourist Information Office.

Adventure Holidays

Centre A

LOCATION   4 miles from Ross-on-Wye in the Wye Valley.

TYPE OF CENTRE   Permanent PGL activity centre.

ACCOMMODATION   Multi-bedded dormitories and 4-berth tents.

FACILITIES   Barn/recreation room, drying room, sick-bay.

ACTIVITY LOCATIONS   On-site within the 6 acres of grounds, in the Wye Valley and the Forest of Dean.

ACTIVITIES   Abseiling, aerial runway, archery, assault course, kayak canoeing, Canadian canoeing, fencing, forest trail, go-karts (July/Aug only), grass skiing, initiative exercises, motorsports, pony trekking, raft building, rifle- shooting, roller skating, sailing, soccer, windsurfing.

Centre B

LOCATION   5 miles from Bideford, North Devon.

TYPE OF CENTRE   Permanent PGL activity centre.

ACCOMMODATION   Multi-bedded dormitories. (Please bring own sleeping bag).

FACILITIES   Lounge, games room, drying room, sick-bay.

ACTIVITY LOCATIONS   On-site within the 22 acres of grounds, on Lake Tamar and the North Devon Coast.

ACTIVITIES   Abseiling, archery, assault course, basketball, Canadian and kayak canoeing, climbing, coastal walk, fencing, motorsports, orienteering, overnight camp, raft building, rifle-shooting, ropes course, sailing, skateboarding, softball, speed-sailing, surfing, volleyball, wave-canoeing and windsurfing.

Centre C

LOCATION   Hindhead in Surrey.

TYPE OF CENTRE   Permanent PGL activity centre.

ACCOMMODATION   Multi-bedded dormitories.

FACILITIES   Indoor rifle range, classrooms, games rooms, hall, drying room, sick-bay.

ACTIVITY LOCATIONS   On-site within the 40 acres and a local forest trail.

ACTIVITIES   Abseiling, archery, arts and crafts, assault course, campcraft, chute games, clay modelling, climbing, fencing, football, forest trail, go-karts, initiative exercises, judo, kite-making, motorsports, mountain bikes, orienteering, overnight camp, pop lacrosse, rifle-shooting, roller skating, softball, tug of war, video filming, volleyball.

In a small group

1 At which of the 3 PGL centres can you do:
   - softball
   - pony trekking
   - video filming
   - sailing?
2 Are these statements true (T), false (F) or is there not enough evidence (NEE)?
   A You can learn to abseil at all 3 centres.
   B All 3 centres offer roller skating.
   C None of the holidays offer hang-gliding.
   D 2 of the centres offer windsurfing.
   E All the centres cater for girls and boys.
3 What do these words or phrases mean?
   - location
   - sick-bay
   - multi-bedded
   - initiative exercises

What to do next

In pairs

Role play a conversation between a person who likes adventure holidays and one who hates them. It might begin something like this:
A We had a great time abseiling.
B Abseiling! You must be mad. You wouldn't catch me hanging off a cliff.

Holiday diary

What to do

On your own

You are on a week's holiday at a PGL centre. You have been there for 4 days and each day you have done something different.

Write a diary entry for these 4 days. If you are really enjoying the week you might start the first entry like this:

Monday 1 July
What a brilliant place. I am learning to canoe...

Or if you are not enjoying it you could begin it like this...

Monday 1 July
I wish I was at home in my nice warm bed. I fell out of my canoe three times today...

Where Are They Going?

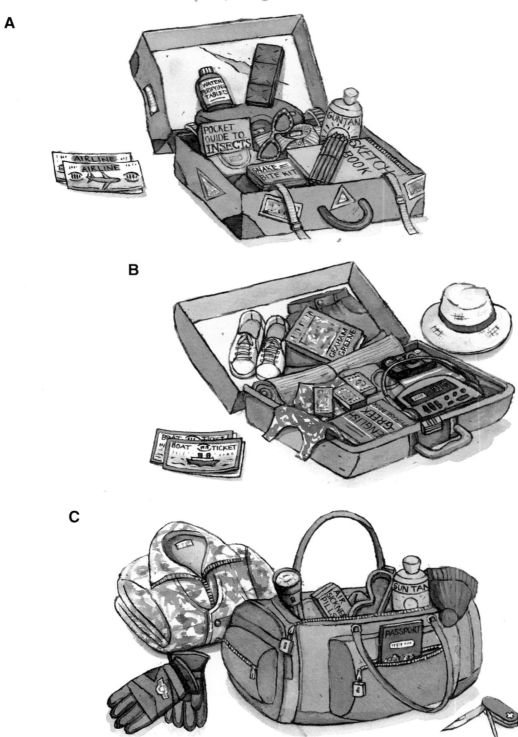

What to do

In pairs

What clues can you find in each case about:
- the sex of the traveller
- how they are going to travel
- the kind of place they are travelling to
- what they will be doing when they get there?

Make a note of these clues for suitcases A and B, and bag C.

What to do next

On your own

You are one of the 3 travellers. You decide to send a postcard to your best friend describing your holiday. Write the postcard. Then draw a picture of what might be on the front of the card, using the clues you have written down already.

Packing your bag

What to do

In pairs

Each pack your own mystery suitcase. Think of an interesting and exciting place to go for a holiday (e.g. The South Pole, Transylvania, Mars) and make a list of things you would need to take with you. Draw an open suitcase and pack it with clues – but do not make them too easy.

Then see if your partner can guess where you are going.

What Do You Like Best?

A Winter ski holiday with school group

B Family seaside holiday in the UK

C Cycling or camping holiday with friends

D Family beach holiday in a hot country

E Holiday with friends in a noisy, busy place with lots to do, like discos

F Active sporting holiday at a leisure park

In pairs

1 Look at photos A-F on page 12 and say if you would like or dislike each kind of holiday. Give reasons. Then make a note of your answers like this:

A *I would like this holiday because I would love to learn to ski.*

2 Think of 2 or 3 things that could happen to spoil each holiday. Could you prevent any of these problems? If so, how?

3 Role play a conversation between a travel agent and a customer whose holiday turned into a nightmare.

What to do next

In a small group

1 Ask 5 or 6 people (family, friends, neighbours) what kind of holidays they like.
Try to interview people who are older and younger than yourself. Find out if they like to go:
- to a new place each year or the same place
- to hot or cool places
- to a city or the country
- abroad or stay at home
- in the winter or summer

Make up 5 questions using the points above.
Question 1 might be:

1 *Do you like to go to the same place each year or somewhere different?*

Think about how you will record the answers. Will you make notes or record the interview on tape?

2 When each group has done their survey, pool all the results. Draw 5 bar charts to show the information you gathered about holidays.
Make a wall display and illustrate it with pictures and maps from travel brochures.

END OF UNIT REVIEW

1

2

Alien

| **SKILLS YOU WILL USE IN THIS UNIT** |
| 1 Reading for enjoyment |
| 2 Drawing and labelling a diagram |
| 3 Thinking about describing words |
| 4 Using a dictionary |
| 5 Discussing opinions |
| 6 Writing a diary entry |

Great Aunt Emma

Great Aunt Emma seems to come from nowhere. She has not been staying with Tim and Beth's family for long, when Beth begins to grow suspicious. Beth is Tim's younger sister. Tim does not always believe everything she says. One day they all go ice-skating and Great Aunt Emma falls over. Tim is writing in his diary what Beth says she saw.

Feb. 9 'Great Aunt Emma was lying on the ground in a heap. She was not groaning or moaning, just lying there and kicking her legs, trying to get up. I went close to her and got hold of her elbow so that I could help pull her up. She did not say anything to me, like "Help me" or "My wrist hurts" – she just tried to get up. When I seized her elbow, I saw her wrist. The hand was dangling. The wrist was so badly broken that the skin was all cut open in a gash and the bones were showing.'

I told Beth I understood all this, but she seemed unwilling to go on. She looked at me and wailed, 'Oh, it's no good, you'll never believe me!' but I made her go on. She said: 'The skin was gashed open but there was no blood. The bones stuck out but they were not made of real bone – they were made of shiny steel!'

I have these words right. Beth did say what I have written. I am quite certain about asking her what sort of

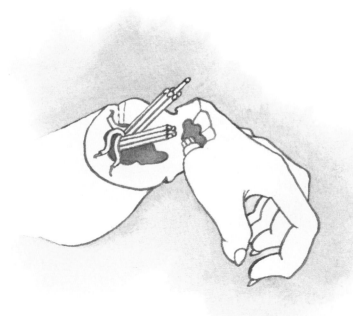

bones, what sort of steel and so on. Her answers were, that the steel was silvery shiny and that the bones looked smaller than proper bones – more like umbrella ribs. When I asked her what umbrella ribs look like, she answered (correctly) that they are made of channels of steel, not solid rods like knitting needles. She said that G.A.E.'s bones were in 'little collections' of these steel ribs and that the skin had been torn by a few of the ribs breaking away from a main cluster and coming through the skin.

So I asked her again about the absence of blood and she was positive. She said there was no blood, no blood at all, the skin was just split open. I asked her what colour the skin was and she said the same colour outside as in. I said, well, there must have been meaty stuff where the bones were, but she said no. There was nothing but the steel ribs and that the skin was just a thick layer 'like the fat on a mutton chop before it is cooked', but with a tear in it.

She began again. 'I saw her wrist mend! I saw it heal itself!' I must say, this gave me goosepimples. I said, 'What do you mean?' and Beth told me that as she watched, the skin came together over the broken bones leaving a bump covering the breaks. 'That's why I can't stand her, BECAUSE SHE'S NOT REAL!' Beth shouted, 'NONE OF HER IS REAL!'

What to do

In pairs

1 Copy the diagram on page 15 onto the middle of a new page. Then use Beth's description to add labels and colour to it.
2 Why do you think Great Aunt Emma did not cry out when she fell?
3 Write down what you think she might have thought to herself after she fell.

> e.g. I wonder if Beth saw everything…

4 Take it in turns to describe Great Aunt Emma and her fall at the ice rink. As you talk, make notes under these headings.
   - What happened
   - What Beth thinks of her
   - What Tim thinks
   - What you think

What to do next

In pairs

1 Complete the following sentence.

> The word 'alien' makes us think of…

2 Look up the word alien in a dictionary. Note down the two different ideas you now have of the word's meaning.
3 Role play an argument about whether or not Great Aunt Emma is an alien.
4 Perform your role play for your class.

More Evidence

Feb. 18 At teatime Mac asked Grinny (our name for G.A.E.) point-blank about earlier days. Where did she spend her childhood, he asked and wouldn't let go.

Mum tried to interrupt by saying something or other, but Mac kept asking. At last Grinny said, 'Oh the past is over and done with, I never think of the past.'

Mac still pressed on and said, 'Oh but surely you must think about your sister, Tim's granny?' Mum sort of gasped and made a face to shut Mac up but Grinny replied, 'Well, you see, my sister and I were so very different. Quite different. Very close, of course, but quite different.' Then she gave a sort of laugh which could have been embarrassment but which Beth later said was sinister. (Beth's new word.)

Mac said, 'But—' again and Mum came in very strong saying, 'Mac, I would rather you didn't pester Aunt Emma with questions.' Now comes the significant part. An hour or more later, I found Mum in the kitchen and said to her, 'Oh, I do wish you had let Mac go on, I was hoping we'd find out.' She said, 'Go on about what?' I said, 'About Aunt Emma's past and about granny and everything.'

She looked me straight in the eye and said, 'What are you talking about? Mac said what?' She did this as though she really meant it – as if she really had forgotten the conversation. But she doesn't forget things, she has the usual terrifying woman's memory about anything to do with people – what they wore, what they said, etc., etc., etc.

Anyhow, I kept on at her a bit more and even said, 'Don't you remember telling us not to pester Aunt Emma with questions about granny?' but either Mum wasn't really hearing me or she was making everything slide out of her mind.

Unless, of course, someone else – Grinny herself! – was making her forget.

Then suddenly Mum looked ill. She put her hand to her head and said, 'I'm so tired. My head aches.'

I have just re-read all this and have realized what a complete fool I am making of myself. Going on like a girl about what this one said and what that one said and if you want my opinion... worse than a girl. And all about a perfectly ordinary old lady.

Nicholas Fisk (from *Grinny*)

What to do

In a small group

1 Look up the meanings of these six adjectives which might describe Tim.

frightened
sexist
imaginative
logical
confused
curious

2 Choose the three words which describe Tim best.
3 Pick one phrase from anywhere in the text which tells you something about Tim's character. Explain what it tells you.

  e.g. Tim describes Grinny as a 'perfectly ordinary old lady.' This shows that he likes to persuade himself everything is really all right.

18

Explanations

A Great Aunt Emma is a robot escaped from a mad scientist who wants to rule the world.

B Great Aunt Emma is a perfectly ordinary old lady who has a bad effect on Beth.

C Great Aunt Emma is a being from another world who plans to change the Earth's future.

What to do

On your own

Which do you think is the most likely explanation, A, B, or C?

Write this down or invent your own explanation. Explain your choice to the class.

What to do next

On your own

Write up Tim's diary entry for the night that he finally realizes the truth about Great Aunt Emma!

Look back to the time when you thought Grinny was 'a perfectly ordinary old lady'. Include your thoughts and feelings about her now.

Try to copy the way Tim writes, as if he is chatting to himself. You might start your diary entry like this:

e.g. *Well, now I've seen it all! At last the truth has been revealed...*

END OF UNIT REVIEW

1

2

Unit 3

Telling the Future

SKILLS YOU WILL USE IN THIS UNIT

1 Reading and thinking about material in magazines
2 Discussion and note-making
3 Writing for a clear purpose
4 Researching information
5 Presenting ideas as a wall display

Looking Ahead

Pisces (Feb 20–Mar 20)

Girls — It isn't going to be easy to fend off the advances of someone you like but don't fancy. In which case you must head straight to a person whom you love and trust for support.

Boys — If one of your parents comes on too strong then you mustn't overreact as it will only lead to another family drama the likes of which you've never seen. Ask someone for advice.

Taurus (Apr 21–May 21)

Girls — Romance is thrust to the very top of your wants list this week. There is no doubt in my mind that whoever casts their peepers on you will be knocked out by your presence.

Boys — You are pretty hip when it comes to anything creative. If you see yourself as a budding artist, sportsman or musician then get your act together now and you are it!

Cancer (June 22–July 23)

Girls — The trouble is if you try getting your own way through a tirade of tears you will only queer your own pitch when you are really upset, then folks'll think you're just trying it on.

Boys — A letter, phone call or visitor is just what you need to bump your life up. Blimey, are you a bored fella? Well the next couple of weeks should really liven up thanks to a new dude.

Russell Grant (from *Fast Forward*)

What to do

In a small group

Ask each member of your group what they think about horoscopes. Record your findings like this:

Name	Main points of what they said
Rita	I never read them, normally. Sometimes I do look to see if what they say fits with what's going on.

What to do next

In a small group

1 Read the magazine horoscopes on pages 20–21.
2 Make notes about them under these headings.
   - The main subject of the horoscopes for Pisces and Taurus boys
   - The main subject of the horoscopes for Pisces and Taurus girls
   - Any other subjects you find in these or other horoscopes
   - The words Russell Grant uses to make the horoscopes seem friendly and chatty, e.g. 'peepers', 'hip'
   - Two examples of the promise of something good
   - Two examples of a warning

SAGITTARIUS *for the week 19–25 August*

1 *Life* It's not the best time to start anything new, so play safe, especially in your social life. Don't try out a new image until you're feeling more confident about yourself.

Love The occasional tiff between you and your guy doesn't have to mean the end of the world, so don't panic over the weekend. You'll have a lot of fun making up afterwards.

Just 17

2 You may have to go back to the beginning to work out what's gone wrong. If it's a love wrangle it may mean backing down. Any sort of applications or competition entries look well starred now. Something that was held up last month should be on the horizon now. That should be a relief.

My Guy

3 *Fun* Not facing up to that pile of work now will only mean late nights and catching up later on. Do it right away and you can enjoy yourself in the future.

Love Go out with him if you want to, but make sure you realize that it could spoil a good friendship. Would things ever be the same if you split up?

Money Work out exactly what you can afford and stick to it. There's no room for any extra spending, that's for sure!

Mates They've been leading you astray lately – and you've been letting them. Stop and think about what you're doing – some time on your own would be a good idea.

Jackie

A

Aug 20th

My Diary

It's not my fault Mum and me are at each other's throats all the time. I always get the blame. As if I'm supposed to know what I've done wrong. I got my membership for the club which should have come last month, that's good. I thought it had got lost in the post.

B

Rifkah's diary KEEP OUT!

Aug 24: I really feel like doing something new. I fancy getting my hair cut like Charlie's, but I'd probably look a right idiot. I've had a lousy weekend. I shouldn't 'ave gone on about his mates like that. Hope we have a good time down at the centre tonight.

C

CONFIDENTIAL INFORMATION!

Aug 22nd I must sort out my project before next week. Why didn't I do it when it was given out? I like Gab as a friend but I dunno about anything else. I don't seem to have done much this summer but hang about my mate's house. And I'm broke!

What to do

On your own

1. Match horoscopes 1, 2, and 3 with diary entries A, B, and C.
2. Make up 2 more situations which would fit this advice from horoscope 2:
   'You may have to go back to the beginning to work out what's gone wrong.'
3. Write a horoscope for this week that includes the sort of subjects found in the examples in this unit.
   Be friendly and chatty towards your reader. Remember to give advice and warnings about what will happen this week.
4. Read your horoscope to the group. Score one point for each thing in your horoscope which fits what has happened to someone in your group.

Horoscopes

Some people believe that the positions of the Sun, Moon, and planets among the stars can be used to make predictions about their lives and characters, and even about world events. The people who make predictions from the stars are called astrologers. A serious astrologer will make a plan of where the Moon, Sun, and planets are at an important time, such as when someone is born, then say what they think it means. The plan is called a horoscope. Astrologers believe that the Sun's position is one of the most important factors. The Sun's path in the sky takes a year to go through the twelve constellations of the zodiac. Your sun sign depends on where the Sun is in the zodiac at the time you are born. Most scientists think that astrology is a superstition and not based on facts. Even so, some people are convinced that it works and have a horoscope cast before making an important decision, like choosing the date of a wedding.

Oxford Children's Encyclopedia

What to do

In a small group

1 Where was the Sun in the zodiac when each of you were born? What is your sign of the zodiac?
2 Name 3 things that some people believe about horoscopes.
3 Use your school or local library to look for more information about astrology and horoscopes. You could start by finding some answers to these questions.
   • When and where did people start believing the 'stars' could tell their future?
   • Which famous people have believed in horoscopes?
   Record your findings in a table like this:

Horoscopes – Did You Know?	
1	Adolf Hitler often took advice from his astrologer instead of his generals.
2	

What to do next

In a small group

Write 4 to 6 sentences explaining what you think about the horoscopes in magazines and newspapers. Use these views as the centre for a wall display about horoscopes and astrology.

This illustration should give you some ideas on what to include in the display and how to present it.

Use a ruler   Make the display colourful   Word process your horoscopes

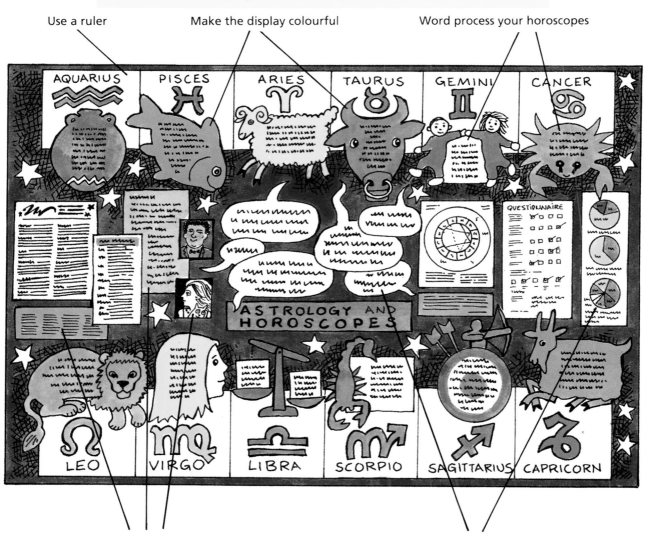

Include cuttings, handwritten pieces, and photos   Arrange your work in an eye-catching way

END OF UNIT REVIEW

1
2

Unit 4

What D'Yer Say?

SKILLS YOU WILL USE IN THIS UNIT

1 Reading a poem aloud and recording it
2 Thinking about the words we use in spoken and written English
3 Writing a dialogue
4 Acting out a scene
5 Planning and writing a poem
6 Giving your opinion

Ta-ra Mam

Ta-ra mam.
Can you hear me? I'm going out to play.
I've got me playing-out clothes on
and me wellies.
What d'yer say?
Oh! I'm going to the cow-field.
I'm going with me mates.
Yes! I know tea's nearly ready.
I promise I won't be late.

Anyway, what we havin'?
Can't I have beans on toast?
What d'yer mean, mam, summat proper?
I ate me dinner (almost).
No, I won't go anywhere lonely,
and I'm going with Chris and Jackie,
so if anyone gets funny
we can all do our karate!

Yer what?
(Oh blimey. Here we go again.)
No, I won't go near the river.
I know we've had too much rain
and I won't go in the newsagent's
trying to nick the sweets.
Yer what, mam? I'm not. Honest.
I'm not trying to give you cheek.

Wait mam.
Hang on a minute. Chris is here in the hall.
He says summat good's on the telly,
so I think I'll stay in after all!

Brenda Leather

What to do

In a small group

Read the poem and discuss the questions below.
1 Where is the child while this 'conversation' is going on?
2 Where do you think 'mam' is?
3 Write a sentence on what the child wants to do in the first verse.
4 Write a sentence on what he or she decides to do in the last verse.
5 How old is the main speaker in the poem? Give a reason for your choice.

> The boy's mam made an appeal for anyone…

6 The poem uses informal words which a TV newsreader would not use. Write down at least 5 of these phrases. Use these phrases to help make a table like the one below.

Informal	Formal
Hang on	Wait

27

One Side of the Conversation

The poem *Ta-ra Mam* is like one side of the conversation between the child and the mother.

What to do

In pairs

1 Copy this table and together fill in the blanks in the left-hand column: Mum's half of the conversation.
2 Try reading aloud what you have got in the table. Mum goes first!

What Mum says	What Child says
Don't get all mucked up. Those shoes cost me a fortune.	I've got me playing-out clothes on and me wellies.
	Oh! I'm going to the cow-field.
	I'm going with me mates.
	Yes! I know tea's nearly ready.
	I promise I won't be late.
All you eat is crisps and other rubbish. I want you to eat summat proper!	What d'yer mean, mam, summat proper? I ate me dinner (almost).
	No, I won't go anywhere lonely, and I'm going with Chris and Jackie.
	No, I won't go near the river and I won't go in the newsagent's trying to nick the sweets.
OK love, see you later. Take care!	Hang on a minute... I think I'll stay in after all.

What to do next

In pairs

1 Practise reading *Ta-ra Mam*. Split it up so that you each read a verse in turn.
   It may help to think about some of the 'Tips for Reading Aloud' shown on page 29, as you practise the poem.
2 Record your reading and then play it back to yourselves. Try recording all or some of the poem again.
   Keep recording the poem until you feel happy with it.

Tips for Reading Aloud

Do I understand all the words?

What kind of voice am I going to use – worried, fed-up?

Which words do I want to stress?

Where do I need to pause or stop?

Do I need to speak some lines faster or slower?

Is it all loud enough?

What to do

In a small group

1 Make a list of all the things that parents worry about when their children go out on their own.
2 Write down as many phrases, which parents say to their children when they are going out, as you can think of.
   e.g. *Have you got money on you? Do be careful!*
3 Role play a scene between parents and a child who is going out.

What to do next

On your own

Write your own poem about what a worried parent says to a child who is going out. Only write the parent's side of the conversation.
   Leave your reader to guess what the child is saying.
Try splitting your poem into verses. As you plan the poem, it may help if you summarize each verse like this:

   e.g. *Verse 1 = What time child will be home and meal times*
   Verse 2 = Where child is going and who with
   Verse 3 = What child will get up to when out

END OF UNIT REVIEW
1
2

Power for Peace

> ### SKILLS YOU WILL USE IN THIS UNIT
>
> 1 Thinking about the structure of a story
> 2 Writing from the viewpoint of one character
> 3 Planning the events in a story
> 4 Drafting a story on a word processor
> 5 Writing with a partner
> 6 Designing a cover for a book

Setting the Scene...

Read this storyboard for the adventure story, *Power for Peace*.
Imagine that you are the main character in the story.

1 When you were five you were sent from your home to live at your eccentric great uncle's house on the other side of town. You were to begin a very special training.

2 Your uncle is old and frail. He is also very wise and the keeper of a secret object of great power. As a young person he travelled to distant places. He is surrounded by mystery.

3 You are being trained to become the guardian of this special object. Whatever 'it' is, it has the power to end conflict and war between different peoples.

4 You have spent nearly ten years developing many different physical and mental powers which no one would suspect you of having.

5 You often wonder what the secret object is. Is it kept in one of the locked rooms? Or is it something that you see every day amongst the many mysterious things in the house?

6 Your uncle is the victim of a serious robbery. 'It' has been stolen along with other things. The shock proves too much for the old man. You arrive on the scene just in time to hear his last words.

Making decisions

As the storyteller and the main character, you will have to make choices and decisions about how the story will develop.

What to do

In a small group

1 Discuss what the secret object could be. Remember, it has such power that it could even end wars. Make a list of your ideas.

> **e.g.** a sapphire ring
> an ancient scroll

2 Decide on 4 physical skills and 4 mental skills that your training has given you to use in the cause of good.
Write these down like this:

Physical	Mental
Can hold breath for long periods of time	Can tell truth from lie

3 Make a list of ideas for a special 'tool' that will help you to find the stolen object.

> **e.g.** a key which will turn any lock
> a wristwatch that can stop time for 10 seconds in every 24 hours

4 Searching through your uncle's belongings you find several things that seem like clues about who has stolen the secret object. Make a list of these.

> **e.g.** a photo taken 15 years ago of your uncle and a woman
> a letter signed by...

Chapter 1

The sun was dancing through a gap in my curtains when I woke up very early the next morning. I quickly got a grip on my first feelings of anger about what had happened the day before. I knew I was going to need all my powers for the great task ahead.

My mind was filled with questions. Did the robbers know what they had taken? Would they just throw it away? What was 'it' anyway? Would this priceless object be sold for peanuts or gather dust for years in somebody's attic? Could its powers be discovered and used for evil purposes?

After hours of meditation some clear pictures began to form in my mind; the first was of a row of black numbers on a yellow background, the second was a rear view of a short-haired woman and the third was of a dingy shop window piled high with junk. I wondered whether any or all of these could be the clues I needed to light my path. My body was crying out for exercise and so I decided to leave these questions until after a late night run.

Outside it was damp and windy but it was good to feel alive as I raced through the empty streets. Suddenly I stopped. It was as if I had run into a sheet of plate glass. I looked around. At first I did not see anything – but then…

Choosing for Chapter 2

A ...through an upstairs window, I saw the back of a closely cropped head.

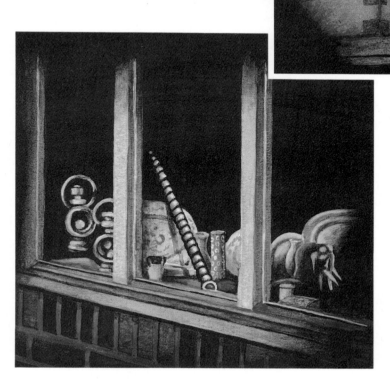

B ...up the alley on my left I saw part of a car number plate.

C ...an object in a shop window on the other side of the road grabbed my attention.

34

What to do

On your own

1 Choose option A, B or C as the event to begin Chapter 2 of *Power for Peace* and write the next stage of the story.
2 End Chapter 2 by listing 3 exciting choices for what might happen at the start of the next chapter.

What to do next

In pairs

1 Swap your work and write Chapter 3 of each other's stories. End this with 3 more choices for what happens next.
2 Next you could add one or more stages to your own story to complete it.

Drafting and revising the story

What to do

In pairs

1 Word process the completed drafts of your joint work. As you do this, decide together if you want to change any details of your stories.
2 Illustrate the scenes you like best.
3 Each present your work as a short book. Write a blurb to go on the back cover which advertises and explains what kind of story it is. Design a front cover, that shows the content and will appeal to readers of your own age.

END OF UNIT REVIEW
1
2

Unit 6

Blitz

SKILLS YOU WILL USE IN THIS UNIT

1 Reading for information
2 Thinking about eyewitness accounts
3 Writing a radio report
4 Writing an eyewitness account

Remembering the Raids

During the Second World War, between September 1940 and May 1941, German planes bombed London and many other British cities. These raids were called 'The Blitz'. Here are three memories of these raids.

A Patricia Brooks was eleven and lived near Croydon. They had a small room under the stairs which her mother was convinced was the safest place to be in an air-raid:

'When the siren sounded my father called us from our beds, complete with blanket and pillow each to settle in for the night. An older sister, who had a small baby, would never respond and my father would keep shouting until she did, hugging the baby. We were all very dopey for lack of sleep and one night when this happened it had been ages before we realized that my sister was hugging and talking quietly to a pillow and Terry, her small son was lying on the floor in the bedroom.

B Kathleen Heavens had an early warning system:

If a bomb was dropping near, our parrot used to turn upside down on her perch yelling 'Ohh!' When we saw her do that we all used to dive for cover under the big double bed.

ST PAUL'S CATHEDRAL

In the event of an **AIR RAID** the Crypt will be open to the Public

C Violet Podger (now Shilling) was twelve and with her fourteen-year-old sister made her way to a brick air-raid shelter:

My mother was expecting a baby so my father made a shelter for her and my two brothers, eleven and nine, in a chalk-pit at the bottom of our garden. So each night we would all go to our separate shelter.

When my sister and I woke up one morning we were informed that my mother had gone into hospital in the night to have her baby.

I went with my sister to tell my dad and he came back to our house, leaving my two brothers in the shelter. The air-raids in those days would start as soon as it got dark and the all clear would sound as soon as it got light.

We went indoors and not long afterwards I heard an aeroplane, so I said to my dad, 'Hark. Here comes a Jerry.' With that he went out to the garden to find my sister. The next thing I remember was the windows rattling and I had all the debris over me. I couldn't move and I could hear people trying to get me out. I was calling out, 'Help! I am here. Here's my arm. Can you see it?'

I was rescued and taken to the local hospital where I received treatment for shock and a slight concussion. I was kept in hospital about a week and kept wondering why no-one came to see me, especially my dad. Then at the end of the week my dad's sister came to see me. She was all in black.

She told me that my dad had been killed, and my sister.

My mum had a daughter the same day.

from *Waiting For the All Clear*

In pairs

1 Discuss and note down which of the memories tell you that people in The Blitz:
   • tried to carry on a normal life
   • were in greater danger at night
   • helped each other
   • did not always go into shelters during the raids
2 What activities that you do now with your friends and family would have been impossible during The Blitz?
3 Who do you think suffered most during The Blitz, the very young or the very old?

Radio reporter

People did not have TV during The Blitz. They listened to the radio all the time to find out what was happening.

In a small group

Write a radio report on the bomb blast that blew the bus into the house.

One person in your group should be the reporter, others can be the people who live in the house, rescue workers, etc.

Use clues from the photograph on page 37 and the memories to help you make the report more detailed. For example, someone who lived in the house might say:

The blast blew me out of bed. I sleep in the front of the house and the wheels came right in through my window!

Write and rehearse what each person will say. Then make a tape recording of the report.

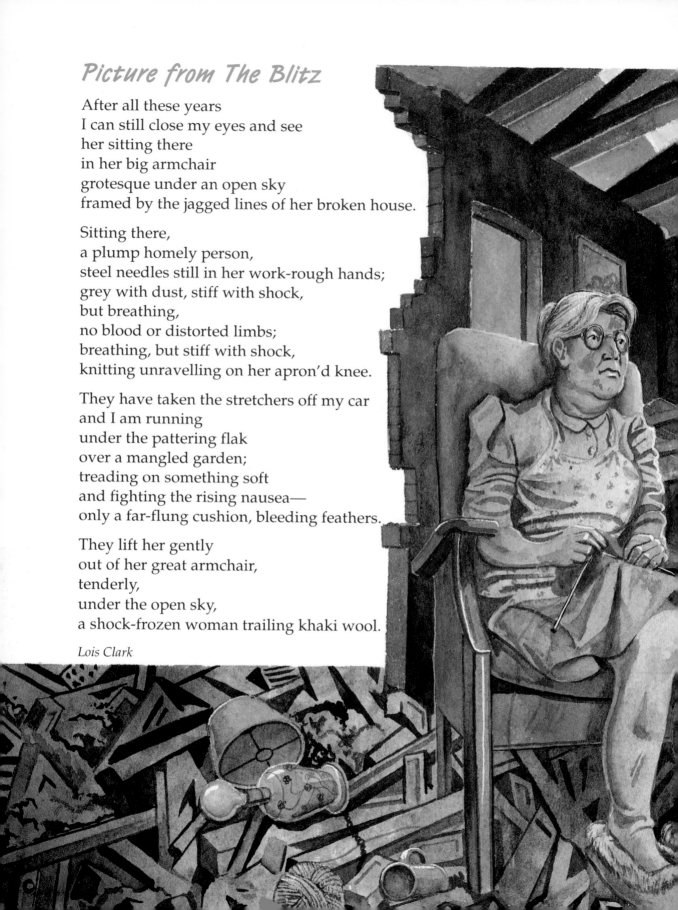

Picture from The Blitz

After all these years
I can still close my eyes and see
her sitting there
in her big armchair
grotesque under an open sky
framed by the jagged lines of her broken house.

Sitting there,
a plump homely person,
steel needles still in her work-rough hands;
grey with dust, stiff with shock,
but breathing,
no blood or distorted limbs;
breathing, but stiff with shock,
knitting unravelling on her apron'd knee.

They have taken the stretchers off my car
and I am running
under the pattering flak
over a mangled garden;
treading on something soft
and fighting the rising nausea—
only a far-flung cushion, bleeding feathers.

They lift her gently
out of her great armchair,
tenderly,
under the open sky,
a shock-frozen woman trailing khaki wool.

Lois Clark

What to do

In pairs

Answer these questions about *Picture from The Blitz*.
Give reasons for your answers.
1 What was the woman doing when the bomb dropped?
2 Was she killed or injured?
3 What does the poem tell you about the woman?
4 Why does the poet still remember the woman 'after all these years'?
5 What was the poet thinking as she ran through the 'mangled garden'?

What to do next

On your own

Imagine that you are the woman in the poem and you are to be interviewed about your experience. Write down notes for what you will say in the interview. The memories on page 36 may help you. You might start something like this:

I was sitting in my favourite armchair when I heard…

END OF UNIT REVIEW
1
2

Unit 7

Just for Laughs

SKILLS YOU WILL USE IN THIS UNIT

1 Writing about your opinions
2 Solving word puzzles
3 Reading for enjoyment
4 Making a storyboard
5 Writing a report

Practical Jokes

Blown Over

Equipment: a large, heavy book, a polythene bag or a balloon.

This trick can also win you money. Stand the large, heavy book on a table and bet someone he can't knock it over by using only his breath. He will huff and puff until he is purple in the face, but won't manage it. Then you can reveal how it is done. Put a polythene bag or a balloon underneath the book, and simply blow into it. As the bag or balloon inflates, the book will start to teeter until, finally, it falls over.

Bun Fight

Equipment: iced buns, an un-iced bun, a tube of toothpaste.

Put the iced buns on a plate, and then get to work on the un-iced bun. Squeeze toothpaste on top of it in a pattern to match the iced buns. If they have a cherry on top, put one on top of the spoof bun, too. It should look exactly the same as the others. Then offer your victim a bun, having arranged the plate so that the spoof bun is likely to be the one taken. Eat a bun yourself, so there is nothing to arouse suspicion. But when the poor victim takes a bite – ugh!

Water Shower

Equipment: a plastic bottle, a pin.

Use a pin to pierce a ring of holes in the bottom of an empty plastic bottle with a tightly fitting cap. Fill the bottle to the brim with water, and screw on the top tightly. Dry the outside of the bottle. While the lid is on, the bottle will not leak. Find a likely victim and tell him that you are having difficulty in unscrewing the cap and ask him to help you. As soon as the top is loosened, water will start to pour through the holes in the bottom of the bottle, wetting your poor victim's feet.

from *Gary Wilmot's Big Book of Practical Jokes*

What to do

In a small group

1 Which of the practical jokes do you each like best? Why?
2 Which joke would be the easiest to do?
3 Which would be the hardest?
4 Do you think any of these tricks might be dangerous?
5 Role play a conversation between a joker and a victim after a practical joke has gone wrong.

What to do next

On your own

Some people think practical jokes are just harmless fun. Others think they are stupid because they can go wrong.
   What do you think?
   Write 4 or 5 sentences about this topic. Start like this:

   e.g. I think practical jokes are harmless fun/dangerous
         because…

43

Letter by Letter

Look at this:

> T4.00pm

What does it mean? Not a lot until you stop to think about it. It's the letter T followed by a time of day. That's it!

> T4.00pm = Tea Time

How about this:

> MAAWNAGYER

It's tricky. Written like this it should be a bit easier.

> MaAwNaGyER

I'll give you a clue. You are looking for the first four words of a famous Christmas carol. Now you see it, don't you?

> MAAWNAGYER = AWAY in a MANGER

This next one is a bit different. What have we here?

> POTOOOOOOOO

Any idea? Set out like this, you may find it easier:

> POT OOOOOOOO

What is it? Pot and then eight Os - yes:

> POTOOOOOOOO = POTATOES

Now you've got the idea, have a go at this. You should get the first one in a flash. (And, yes, that is a clue.)

> BOLT
> TH

Gyles Brandreth (from *A Riot of Riddles*)

In pairs

1 Match puzzles 1–8 with answers A–H.
2 Explain each puzzle to your partner or teacher.

Answers

A flash in the pan
B you are under arrest
C going round in circles
D disinfectant
E a square meal
F backache
G a bedspread
H once upon a time

Mystery riddle

The Case of the Two Butchers

There were two butchers standing behind the counter in a shop. One butcher is short and the other is tall. The tall butcher is the father of the short butcher, but the short butcher is not the son of the tall butcher. How are they related?

Gyles Brandreth (from *A Riot of Riddles*)

In a small group

1 Work out the answer to this mystery riddle.
2 What kind of trick does the story use?
3 Do you know any more riddles like this one? If so, share them with your group.

'What on earth…' said Wally Pratt entering the kitchen, 'is that?!'

'Don't be a wally Wally – it's obvious what it is, it's an off-road scrambling motor bike,' replied his mother. She wiped her forehead with an oily rag and patted the saddle of the vicious looking machine with pride. 'It's only taken me a week to build. It's got long-reach hydraulic front forks and overhead cams; it'll be just the job for next Saturday. Look.'

She pointed to a headline in the evening paper:

> GRAND CROSS-COUNTRY
> MOTOR BIKE SCRAMBLE –
> FIRST PRIZE £500

'Now then Wally, don't just stand there like a blancmange with a headache, help me dry up these carburettors and things, then you can go out and play with your ghastly little friends.'

'I don't know, kids today,' thought Vera, 'when I was his age I could change the big ends on a lorry before breakfast…'

While Vera Pratt was thinking these thoughts Captain Smoothy-Smythe, down at the ABC Garage was having a meeting with his men. In case you haven't met them before they are his chief partner-in-crime, Dud Cheque, and his mechanics, Slimey and Grimey, the O'Reilly brothers.

'Right chaps,' said the Captain. 'There's five hundred quid to be won at this cross-country scramble on Saturday and I intend to win it. Let me test you. Who do you think our main opposition will be?'

'Mrs Pratt, Guv,' said Dud Cheque. 'She always is.'

'Correct, Cheque,' snapped the Captain. 'Thank heavens you are not quite as thick as you look.'

'Ta very much, Guv,' said Dud, pleased with himself.

'So, what are we going to do about it?' asked the Captain, eyeing each man in turn.

'Should we nobble her, sir?' suggested Grimey O'Reilly.

'Nobble her? Of course we'll blinking nobble her!!' roared the Captain. 'She will need to meet with an unfortunate accident that will put the old girl out of action for a long time, a very long time. Look at this map.'

The Captain took out a large map and spread it on his desk. 'My military experience in the war taught me the need for thorough planning. I've studied the course of the race, and I believe that the best point for strategic unsaddling of Mrs Blasted Pratt will be here, very near the end, where this narrow dirt track goes through this gateway.' He pointed to a spot on the map. 'That's Dungy Dell, on the edge of Old Codger's Wood, near where Shady keeps his cattle,' said Grimey O'Reilly.

'Correct. Now then,' continued the Captain firmly. 'You Slimey, will be my race mechanic, and will come to the pits with me. You Cheque, with Grimey, will be in charge of Mrs Pratt's unfortunate accident at the gate. You will achieve it with the help of this...'

The Captain reached down behind him and lifted a huge box on to the desk top. On the side of it were printed the words:

DAISY MOO COW –
GENUINE PANTOMIME COW COSTUME
complete with realistic udder
and swivelling eyes.

'What the heck are we going to do with that, Guv?' said Dud Cheque, wiping his nose on the sleeve of his jacket in amazement.

'Listen carefully, and I'll tell you, idiots!' said the Captain, and he lowered his voice so that only the three of them could hear his fiendish plan...

Brough Girling

In pairs

1 Discuss what the extract tells you about Vera Pratt?
2 What does it tell you about Captain Smoothy-Smythe?
3 Why does the Captain want to 'nobble' Vera?
4 Why do you think the Captain wants a cow costume?
5 Do you think the Captain's plan will work? Give reasons.

What to do next

On your own

Write the next part of the story. Try to think of an incident that involves Vera, the Captain and his crew, as well as the pantomime cow.

Plan out the main events in a storyboard, like the one below, before you start to write. It may also help to draw a map of the race course.

Slimey and the Captain wait to hear from Dud. (Slimey and Grimey are twins)

Dud and Grimey arrive at the gate.

Dud and Grimey get changed into Pantomime cow costume.

Vera can't wait for the race to start.

Dracula's School Report

THE
VAMP HIGHER SCHOOL
TRANSYLVANIA

Name of Pupil: Dracula, Count   Age: 13
Subject: Attendance and punctuality

Dracula's punctuality is appalling. What is the matter with the boy, can't he get up in the morning? To look at him, you would think he had been out all night.

I'm sure his health is suffering. He must get up so late he can't possibly have had time for a bite to eat.

Yesterday he missed the annual cricket match against our deadly rivals, Frankenstein's Middle School - a match we need not have lost had it not been for his absence. It made my blood boil, I can tell you. What chance have you got without your opening bat?

I really wonder whether Dracula's heart is in his school work. Does he not realize what is at stake? He makes me very cross. Unless he starts to put in a lot of effort he will end up without any qualifications at all; what a sucker he'll look then.

No, things must improve immediately. Every member of staff is fed up to the back teeth with Dracula's lateness. It used to be regarded as just a pain in the neck, but no longer. It's now a matter of grave concern.

I want to see him change! Overnight!

Brunhilde Sauerkraut

Brunhilde Sauerkraut
Form Mistress

Michael Coleman

What to do

In a small group

There are many vampire jokes hidden in Dracula's school report, e.g. '...can't possibly have had time for a bite to eat!'
    Make a list of as many as you can find.

What to do next

On your own

Write a school report for one of these characters:

- Batman
- Wonder Woman
- Cinderella
- James Bond
- Robin Hood
- Tutankhamun

Remember to include details of his or her character, what they do, and how they get on with people at school.

END OF UNIT REVIEW

1
2

Our Day Out

> **SKILLS YOU WILL USE IN THIS UNIT**
>
> 1 Reading for enjoyment
> 2 Reading a play extract aloud
> 3 Improvising a scene
> 4 Writing a scene in playscript

At the Zoo

Two teachers, Mr Briggs and Mrs Kay have taken a group of pupils on a trip to the zoo. Read the playscript as a class.

Briggs: And a brown bear is an extremely dangerous animal. You see those claws, they could leave a really nasty mark.

Andrews: Could it kill y' sir?

Briggs: Well why do you think they keep it in a pit?

Ronson: I think that's cruel sir. Don't you?

Briggs: Not if it's treated well, no. Don't forget, Ronson that an animal like this would have been born into captivity. It's always had walls around it so it won't know anything other than this sort of existence, will it?

Ronson: I'll bet it does.

Girl 2:   How do you know? Sir's just told you hasn't he? If it was born in a cage an' it's lived all its life in a cage well it won't know any different will it? So it won't want anything different.

Ronson: Well why does it kill people then?

Andrews: What's that got to do with it, dick head?

Ronson: It kills people because people are cruel to it. They keep it in here, in this pit so when it gets out it's bound to go mad an' want to kill people. Can't y' see?

Andrews: Sir he's thick. Tell him to shuttup.

Ronson: I'm not thick. Even if it has lived all its life in there it must know musn't it sir?

Briggs: Know what Ronson?

Ronson: Know about other ways of livin'. About bein' free. Sir it only kills people 'cos they keep it trapped in here but if it was free an' it was treated all right it'd start to be friends with y' then wouldn't it? If y' were doin' nothing wrong to it it wouldn't want to kill y'.

Briggs: Well I wouldn't be absolutely sure about that, Ronson.

Andrews: Sir's right. Bears kill y' 'cos it's in them to kill y'.

Girl 1: Ah come on sir, let's go to the Pets Corner.

Andrews: No way sir, let's see the big ones.

Briggs: We'll get round them all eventually.

Girl 2: Come on sir, let's go to the Pets Corner...

(Girl 1 and Girl 2 go to link Briggs' arms. He shrugs them off.)

Briggs: Now walk properly, properly...

Girl 1: Agh hey sir, all the other teachers let y' link them.

(Mrs Kay enters with another group of Kids. She has got Kids on either side, linking her arms.)

Mrs Kay: How are you getting on? Plying you with questions?

Briggs: Yes, yes they've been... very good.

Mrs Kay: I'm just going for a cup of coffee. Want to join me?

Briggs: Well I was just on my way to the Pets Corner...

Andrews: It's all right sir, we'll go on our own.

Mrs Kay: Oh come on, they'll be all right.

Briggs: But can these people be trusted Mrs Kay?

Mrs Kay: They'll be all right. Colin and Susan are walking round. And the place is walled in.

Andrews: Go on sir, you go an' have a cuppa. You can trust us.

Briggs: Ah can I though? If I go off for a cup of tea with Mrs Kay, can you people be trusted to act responsibly?

Kids: Yes sir.

Jimmy: Sir what sort of bird's that sir?

Briggs: Erm. Oh let me see, yes it's a macaw.

Mrs Kay: Come on.

Briggs: (*Following Mrs Kay*) They're very good talkers.
(*Mrs Kay and Briggs off.*)

Kevin: I told y' it wasn't a parrot.

Jimmy: (*Trying to get the bird to talk*) Liverpool, Liverpool. Come on say it, y' dislocated sparrow.

Kids: (*Sing*)
Mountain lions and panthers
Leopards in the zoo
What do lions eat?

Jimmy:
Kev: } Evertonians
Kids:

Who's watching who's watching, who's watching who?
Who's watching who's watching who's watching who?

(Mrs Kay and Briggs sitting as if in the cafe, two teas and a couple of cakes. Kids as though looking through the windows of the cafe.)

Kids: Teachers in the cafe
Takin' tea for two
What do they eat

(Spoken) Ogh, chocolate cream cakes!

(Briggs and Mrs Kay suddenly noticing hungry eyes on their cakes.)

Mrs Kay: *(Waving them away)* Ogh go on, go away... shoo...

Kids: *(Dispersing and going off singing)*
Who's watching who's watching who's watching who
Who's watching who's watching who's watching who?

Briggs: Another tea Mrs Kay?

Mrs Kay: Oh call me Helen. Do you know I loathe being called Mrs Kay. Do you know I tried to get the kids to call me by me first name. I told them, call me Helen, not Mrs Kay. They were outraged. They wouldn't do it. So it's good old Mrs Kay again. Oh, no, no more tea thanks.

Briggs: They're really quite interested, the kids, aren't they?

Mrs Kay: In the animals, oh yes. And it's such a help having you here because you know so much about this sort of thing.

Briggs: Well I wouldn't say I was an expert but... you know, perhaps when we're back at school I could come along to your department and show some slides I've got.

Mrs Kay: Would you really? Oh Mr Briggs, we'd love that.

Briggs: Well look, I'll sort out which free periods I've got and we'll organize it for then.

(Colin and Susan approaching. The Kids quickly lined up in the sort of orderly queue Briggs would approve of.)

Susan: Ready when you are.

Mrs Kay: Are they all back?

Susan: It's amazing, we came round the corner and they're all there, lined up waiting to get on the bus.

Mrs Kay: Wonders will never cease.

Briggs: OK. *(Sees the Kids)* Well look at this Mrs Kay, they're learning at last eh? Right, all checked and present? On board then...

(The Kids go to climb aboard just as an Animal Keeper, all polo-neck and wellies, rushes towards them.)

Keeper: Hold it right there.

Mrs Kay: Hello, have we forgotten something?

Keeper: Are you supposed to be in charge of this lot?

Mrs Kay: Why, what's the matter?

Keeper: Children? They're not bloody children, they're animals. It's not the zoo back there, this is the bloody zoo, here.

Briggs: Excuse me! Would you mind controlling your language and telling me what's going on?

Keeper: *(Ignores him, pushes past and confronts the Kids)* Right, where are they?

(Innocent faces and replies of 'What?', 'Where's what?')

Keeper: You know bloody well what...

Briggs: *(Intercepting him)* Now look, this has just gone far enough. Would you...

(He is interrupted by the loud clucking of a hen. The Keeper strides up to a Kid and pulls open his jacket. A bantam hen is revealed.)

Keeper: *(Taking the hen, addresses the other Kids)* Right, now I want the rest.

(There is a moment's hesitation before the floodgates are opened.

Animals appear from every conceivable hiding-place.)

Briggs: *(Glares as the animals are rounded up. The Kids stay in place, waiting for the thunder.)*

Briggs: I trusted you lot. And this is the way you repay me. *(Pause as he fights to control his anger.)* I trusted all of you but it's obvious that trust is something you know nothing about.

Ronson: Sir we only borrowed them.

Briggs: *(Screaming)* Shut up lad! Is it any wonder that people won't do anything for you? The moment we start to treat you like real people, what happens? Well that man was right. You act like animals, animals.

Mrs Kay: Come on now, take the animals back.

(The Kids relieved at finding a way to go. As they move off Briggs remains.)

Briggs: And that's why you're treated like animals, why you'll always be treated like animals.

Kids: *(Sing very quietly as they exit)*
Our day out
Our day out

Briggs: *(Alone on stage)* ANIMALS!
(Blackout.)

Willy Russell (from *Our Day Out*)

In pairs

1 What can you tell about Ronson from the conversation he has with Mr Briggs about the brown bear?
2 What can you tell about Andrews?
3 What do the pupils think of Mrs Kay?
4 How do they behave towards Mr Briggs?
5 Who is to blame for the incident at the Pets' Corner?
6 Is Ronson being serious when he says, 'Sir we only borrowed them'?
7 What does Briggs mean when he says, 'The moment we start to treat you like real people...You act like animals.'?
8 How does Mrs Kay try to calm the situation?

The right stress

Here are some lines from the extract. The underlined words are the ones the actors could stress (say strongly) to get across a certain meaning.

Briggs: And a brown bear is an <u>extremely</u> dangerous animal. You see those claws, they could leave a <u>really</u> nasty mark.
Andrews: Could it <u>kill</u> y' sir?
Briggs: Well why do you think they keep it in a <u>pit</u>?
Ronson: I think that's <u>cruel</u> sir. Don't you?

In a small group

Choose a short section of the extract to read aloud. Try to put the stress on certain words, like the examples above.

If you stress the right words your reading should sound more natural, like speech.

In a small group

What do you think might happen if the group of pupils visited one of these places? Choose one and role play a scene.
- a chocolate factory
- a haunted house
- a fast food restaurant

How scripts are set out

Keeper: *(Ignores him, pushes past and confronts the Kids)* Right, where are they?

(Innocent faces and replies of 'What?', 'Where's what?')

Keeper: You know bloody well what...

Briggs: *(Intercepting him)* Now look, this has just gone far enough. Would you...

(He is interrupted by the loud clucking of a hen. The Keeper strides up to a Kid and pulls open his jacket. A bantam hen is revealed.)

Keeper: *(Taking the hen, addresses the other Kids)* Right, now I want the rest.

(There is a moment's hesitation before the floodgates are opened. Animals appear from every conceivable hiding-place.)

Briggs: *(Glares as the animals are rounded up. The Kids stay in place, waiting for the thunder.)*

Briggs: I trusted you lot. And this is the way you repay me. *(Pause as he fights to control his anger.)* I trusted all of you but it's obvious that trust is something you know nothing about.

Ronson: Sir we only borrowed them.

Briggs: *(Screaming)* Shut up lad! Is it any wonder that people won't do anything for you? The moment we start to treat you like real people, what happens? Well that man was right. You act like animals, animals.

Mrs Kay: Come on now, take the animals back.

(The Kids relieved at finding a way to go. As they move off Briggs remains.)

Briggs: And that's why you're treated like animals, why you'll always be treated like animals.

Kids: *(Sing very quietly as they exit)*
    Our day out
    Our day out

Briggs: *(Alone on stage)* ANIMALS!
    (Blackout.)

Tells the actor who is speaking what to do.

This line is unfinished because the next speaker buts in.

Directions for actors who are not speaking at this time.

Tells the actor how to say the lines.

Direction for lighting crew.

What to do

In a small group

1 Write a scene for a school play involving a teacher and 3 or 4 pupils. You could use the situation you role played on page 56. Set the scene out like the extract above. Use stage directions to show how your actors speak and move.

2 Rehearse your script and make a tape or video recording.

END OF UNIT REVIEW
1
2

Unit 9

Pets Across the World

SKILLS YOU WILL USE IN THIS UNIT

1 Reading different facts and opinions

2 Discussing and comparing points of view

3 Gathering information from a number of sources

4 Conducting an interview

Pets Facts

Pet animal kept in the home to give pleasure

Harraps Easy English Dictionary

Pet an animal that is tamed and treated with affection, kept for companionship or amusement

Oxford Paperback Dictionary

In 1974 there were only 14 Shar-pei known to survive. By 1984 there were 4,000.
Do you think its coat would cause the dog or its owners any problems?

This 'brown' sphinx has very short suede-like hair. This cat is also whiskerless! Cold weather can cause it to catch serious colds.

RSPCA figures, 1989
(for adult dogs and cats)

	Found new homes	*Humanely destroyed*
Dogs	44,600	42,700
Cats	38,300	21,400

Number of calls to RSPCA about cruelty
1989: 1,053,360
1990: 1,162,219

'What makes people take in animals on a whim and then turn them out a few days, weeks or even years later? A pet, whether it is a dog, cat, rabbit, gerbil, budgie or horse, is something that lives and breathes and is dependent on us humans. In return we often receive continuing loyalty and affection.'

(The General Secretary of the Animal Welfare Trust)

In this country there seem to be extremes of kindness and cruelty. Some people seem to believe they have a right to keep animals and they don't always think about whether or not they are able to look after a pet properly. On the whole Britain tends to be a country of animal collectors not lovers. People want fashionable pets. I see the business of dog breeding as a big problem. Nobody wants the stray mongrels and people complain when we have to put them down.

(Nick Welch RSPCA Inspector)

What to do

In a small group

Read the information on these pages. Using this, list 2 or 3 ideas under each of these headings. Include ideas from your own experience of pets as well.
- Keeping Unusual Pets or Rare Breeds
- Why People Abandon Cats and Dogs
- Different Types of Pet Kept in Britain

Pets Abroad

Read these two very different accounts of the pets and animals found in Corfu and China. As you read, remember that Michalis and Huang Wang are not native speakers of English.

My little friends

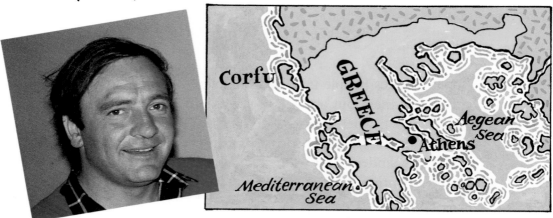

My name is Michalis Mouzakitis. I come from the Greek island of Corfu. Because it's an island there aren't any big wild animals – just things like foxes, snakes, and tortoises. Things have changed a lot in the past 15 years because people travel much more now. Things move from one country to another.

People make money with the tourist now but a lot of people in the villages, like my mother, keep animals like chickens and sheep to give food. People do keep dogs and cats, mainly for hunting and guarding. Dogs live outside – they have places they can go in to shelter. But the sheep we bring them inside in the winter to keep them warm. When I first came to England I was very surprised to see sheep left outside in the snow and I had never seen a dog sitting on a chair or sleeping on a bed!

As I say, things move from one country to another. Last year I saw someone walking a dog on a lead in Corfu town. Everybody looked. They thought it was funny, putting a dog on a lead. Dogs in Corfu have always been big and of no special breed but some people do now have special breed dogs, like the police dogs in England and they have little dogs.

People do keep birds in a cage because they look pretty

and sing. These birds usually come from Africa and you get them in the pet shop in Corfu town. There isn't really a word which means 'pet' in my language but people would say things like 'filos' – 'My little friends'.

When I was a boy we used to bring home little animals. We used to bring home a tortoise and make it a little house or maybe a little bird which we would feed till it grew big. Sometimes the boys used to catch, I forget what you call them now, a sort of flying beetle which glows. They used to tie strings round the middle and the beetles would fly around. I haven't seen this for about 20 years now. Maybe they have gone because of spraying the crops? Children don't seem to make and do things now like they used to. I think this is because of the plastic things they play with. There never used to be any plastic on Corfu.

Walking the birds

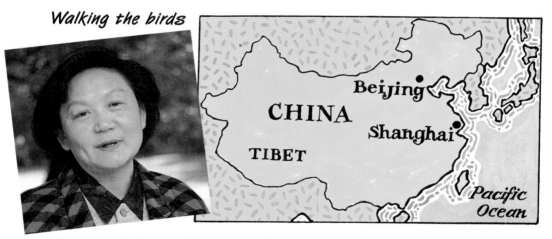

My name is Huang Wang and I come from Shanghai City in China. Because China is such a big country we have many kinds of animals. In the north you can find tigers, leopards, and bears, in the south crocodiles and many kinds of birds. In the west you can find pandas. In the cities people usually keep cats but not many people keep dogs.

It is not a tradition to keep dogs here in Chinese cities, although nowadays rich people have started keeping posh dogs which are very rare in China. There isn't really enough space in cities to keep dogs and it is so expensive to feed them. I was very surprised by the number and different sizes of dogs in Britain.

Many of the retired people in the cities keep birds. They have a great enthusiasm for them. They take their birds to the park in the morning and hang the cages on the branches of the trees. The people make comparisons between the birds and swap ideas. While they are chatting under the trees the birds above are joining in the chorus. Young people do this as well but not so many as the retired people, because they have more time.

When I was a girl very many children used to keep silk-worms for fun. It's a lot of fun watching the silk-worm weave its thread. You have to go and look for or buy mulberry leaves for the silk-worms to eat. They weave a cone of silk around them. Sometimes the cones are white and sometimes a rare yellowish colour. Children keep the cones in their toybox. Not so many children do this now because the leaves are more difficult to find and they have different kinds of entertainment like television and school activities.

People in China do have a passion for their cats and their birds but on the whole they do not feel so strongly about their pets as the British people seem to. There isn't really a word which means 'pet' in the area where I come from. We would just say we 'keep a cat'.

What to do

On your own

Match each animal A-I with Corfu, China, or Britain.

   e.g. C = Britain

On your own

1 Copy and complete this table. Write down what you have learnt about each subject listed in the left-hand column.

	Corfu	Shangai
Location	Small island with one town	Big city in huge country
Birds		
Dogs		
Wild Animals		
Animals used for food		

2 Write about two things which have changed about pets and animals in Corfu and Shanghai.

What to do

In pairs

Read Michalis' and Huang's accounts again. Decide on the 5 questions they were asked to get them to talk about pets.

> e.g. 1 What kind of things have surprised you about animals in Britain?

What to do next

In pairs

1 Take it in turns to interview each other about animals. Start by writing down questions to help you find out your partner's ideas about these topics:
- caring for pets
- cruelty to pets
- bloodsports
- favourite animals

2 Record your interviews on video or tape cassette. During the interview, encourage your partner to say more by nodding, looking at them and agreeing. Play back the tape and write 4 or 5 sentences about how the interview went and how it might be improved.
Tape all or part of the interview again.

END OF UNIT REVIEW

1
2

Oxford University Press, Walton Street, Oxford OX2 6DP

Oxford New York
Athens Auckland Bangkok Bombay
Calcutta Cape Town Dar es Salaam Delhi
Florence Hong Kong Istanbul Karachi
Kuala Lumpur Madras Madrid Melbourne
Mexico City Nairobi Paris Singapore
Taipei Tokyo Toronto

and associated companies in
Berlin Ibadan

Oxford is a trade mark of Oxford University Press

© Selection and Activities Chris Culshaw and Jill Dodgson 1994
First published by Oxford University Press 1994
Reprinted 1995

ISBN 0 19 831431 0

Cover illustration by Alan Nanson

Printed in Hong Kong

In the same series:

Headwork Book 1	0 19 833372 2
Headwork Book 2	0 19 833373 0
Headwork Book 3	0 19 833374 9
Headwork Book 4	0 19 833375 7
Headwork Book 5	0 19 833387 0
Headwork Book 6	0 19 833388 9
Headwork Book 7	0 19 833389 7
Headwork Book 8	0 19 833390 0
English Headwork Book 1	0 19 833376 5
English Headwork Book 2	0 19 833377 3
English Headwork Book 3	0 19 833378 1
English Headwork Book 4	0 19 833379 X
Headwork Stories Book 1	0 19 833380 3
Headwork Stories Book 2	0 19 833381 1
Headwork Stories Book 3	0 19 833391 9
Headwork Stories Book 4	0 19 833392 7
Headwork Anthologies Book 1	0 19 833396 X
Headwork Anthologies Book 2	0 19 833397 8
Headwork Anthologies Book 3	0 19 833398 6